Are You Ready to Make
The Mindset Shift?

The Mindset Shift

Goal Setting Success Secrets

by

Amanda Ollier

&

Chris and Susan Beesley

Copyright 2013 Amanda Ollier and Chris and Susan Beesley.

Discover other titles in this series and other titles by Amanda Ollier at Amazon.

You can also find this book as a Kindle version at Amazon.

All rights reserved.

No part of this document may be reproduced or transmitted in any form or by any means, electronic, mechanical, photocopying, recording, or otherwise, without prior written permission of Amanda Ollier or Chris and Susan Beesley.

Contents

Getting Started	11
The Secret Key to Great Goals	14
When Is the Right Time to Start?	18
Exercise	21
Making Resolutions	26
Why Resolutions Don't Last	29
Why Goals Are Different	32
The Formula for Success	34
Step 1 Change Your Thinking	37
Examples	41
Step 2 Decide Where to Start	43
Choosing Your Key Life Areas	44
Exercise	44
Step 3 Decide Specifically What You Want	
Step 4 The Construction Process	48
Example	50
The Keys to a Compelling Goal	56
Exercise	56
Exercise	58

Setting the Scene	**63**
The Checklist	*63*
Example	*65*
Step 5 Write It All Down	**68**
Example	*70*
Step 6 Follow It Up	**76**
About the Authors	**86**
Amanda Ollier	**86**
Chris and Susan Beesley	**88**
Connect With the Authors Online	**92**
Other Books We've Written	**93**
….And Finally	**94**

Dedication

This book is not only dedicated to you, it **was written for you.**

Our intention in writing this book, is to remind you just how important your reason why is and to give you a system to create the goals that will motivate and drive you to success.

"You become what you think about most" - The Secret

Acknowledgements

Thank you to everyone who has contributed to the creation of this book by giving us their valuable time, energy, inspiration and feedback. Thanks also for confirming to us that we were on the right track and creating something of real worth.

We appreciate you all!

Goal Setting Success Secrets

By Amanda Ollier

&

Chris and Susan Beesley

Getting Started

We've all heard how easy it is to make money on the internet so why is it that so many people fail at the first hurdle? If it wasn't possible to make money on the internet then there wouldn't be so many success stories.

Let's look at how a positive mindset and belief in yourself will help. If you don't think you can do it then you won't. It's as simple as that. Working on the internet is no different to starting any other business. If you have a positive mindset then you have already seen yourself succeeding, so you will.

How Do You Keep that Positive Mindset?

Well, it doesn't happen overnight. You need to have access to positive and inspiring people, and read and listen to people of influence such as Anthony Robbins. Positive mindset can be learnt but it takes practice.

Furthermore, you don't have to be super intelligent or have exceptional talents to achieve success. In fact, if you look at some of the most successful entrepreneurs in the world such as Richard Branson you will find they were not super intelligent or super talented. They just had a very positive outlook on life and a mindset for achievement.

What Is the Secret?

It all starts with Goal Setting. One of the things we notice both professionally and personally, is people often worry that things might go wrong, or put themselves down when things don't go to plan, but they rarely celebrate successes. They say to themselves, 'well I made a mess of that', 'that didn't go very well' or something along those lines. In a way they set themselves up to fail as they don't give themselves a pat on the back or a positive affirmation.

Everyone has goals, aims or objectives they strive to meet in their work or in life in general, whether these are conscious or not. You may want to earn more money, drive a bigger car, have a nicer house or just enjoy your life and work.

But without a clear plan or strategy to get there, it makes it more difficult to achieve. We know from experience that it is easy to drift along, but if you make conscious decisions in your life, you can live one that is inspired and that you enjoy. Using a personal example, when we were writing our book, many people said to us that they want to do the same one day, but by setting our goals, we achieved what we set out to achieve.

The Secret Key to Great Goals

We'd like to begin this book, by sharing with you, the secret to creating the most powerful goals possible. The difference that will make a difference to your life, once you become aware of it.

It's not something original, Abraham Maslow talked about it 70 years ago, Eastern religions have talked about it for ever, and Napoleon Hill described it in very practical terms in his classic book 'Think and Grow Rich', almost 80 years ago.

So, original no, but essential yes!

Maslow talked of Self Actualisation, and Hill of the Definite Purpose or Chief Aim in Life, you can call it what you like as long as you know what yours is! It's covered in Step 3 of this process but it's so important we want you to begin your journey with this end in mind.

When you are thinking about what you want from life, in any area, you must think above and beyond the obvious and tangible, because the real drivers are not found in these. You won't be nearly as motivated by a 'thing' as you will by what that thing might give you, that's where the real power lies in goal setting.

For example; Yes you might want more money - but only because that's a vehicle to something else. It might mean an end to financial worries, physical hardship, a feeling of missing out, or being inferior or hard done by. Having lots of money can solve all those problems, but it's what it will bring you in return that will drive you to seek opportunities to draw it into your life. Having financial abundance is often more about freedom than anything else.

- Freedom to choose how you spend your time and who with
- Freedom to go where you want when you want to
- Freedom to live your life according to your own agenda

- Freedom to do what you want without having to worry about how to pay for it
- Freedom to help others without having to count the cost first
- Freedom to live in the moment

Look for the end result, the ultimate benefit that you will enjoy when you achieve your goal. That is the true secret to goal setting.

Keep asking yourself why you want it.

"What will that give me?"

"What will that allow me to do?"

And make each answer, bigger, better and more abstract than the last.

Keep asking until the only answer you can give sounds so audacious and wonderful and awe inspiring that you want to cry or jump for joy and when you get this far, you'll know you've got to the REAL reason that you want that 'thing'.

Then you will be ready to think about setting goals that will inspire you so much that achieving them is no longer a possibility, it is an inevitability!

"Nature wraps up in the impulse of strong desire "that something" which recognises no such word as impossible, and accepts no such reality as failure."

Napoleon Hill. Think and Grow Rich

~~~

When Is the Right Time to Start?

If you look to external sources for your cue as to when is the 'right time' to do something, like making resolutions at New Year, giving up bad habits at Lent, starting diets on Monday or after the party season, you may think you are just waiting for the time to be *right*, or until that mythical moment when you'll have *spare time* on your hands.

But in truth, you are just putting off until tomorrow what you cannot face today and, if you're not really careful, years of your life will slip by without you ever *finding the right time*.

Why? Because other things will always come along and if you're taking the lead from things outside of yourself, you will always put them first. Your spare time will be filled before you've even noticed you had any!

If you want a better life, then you are going to have to <u>make</u> the time and right now is the perfect time for you to take the decision to map out the future you want, the life you desire and deserve and the success which can so easily be yours.

You have the right and the power to lead your perfect life.

The Reverend Jesse Jackson, American Civil Rights Leader and politician famously said;

"If my mind can conceive it, and my heart can believe it, I know I can achieve it."

And the same is true for you! If you can come up with an idea of how you would like your life to be, with a little help and guidance, we know it really is possible for you to have exactly what you want!

You might not know how to achieve it right now, you might not believe it's possible at the moment either, but both of those are things are changeable.

You didn't know how to walk or talk once upon a time, so you learned by copying others. When you started a new job, sport or hobby, you didn't know all you do now, but you learned, and as you learned, so your beliefs about what you were capable of changed.

~~~

Exercise

Think of something you believe that you are really good at. It can be anything - work related, a hobby, something you like doing, something other people tell you you're good at – anything as long as you feel that it is something you do well.

Now cast your mind a little further back into the past, before you knew how to do that thing so well.

Remember the time before you got so good at it. Remember how you thought about that thing then and answer the following questions.

* How did you feel when you thought about it back then?

* What things did you say to yourself in your head about it?

* Did you believe you'd ever be able to do it without thinking so hard, or feeling nervous beforehand?

* Did you ever dare dream that you'd be so clever?

Probably not; and yet here you are now, knowing and therefore believing that this is something you can now do, and do well.

Many things in life seem so big and unattainable at first, that you might be too intimidated to even begin thinking about how you could achieve them.

Perhaps you have a history that has set you up to expect little of life and/or yourself.

Maybe your self esteem is a bit fragile, or you have tried things before and got your fingers burnt and now feel it's safer not to even try.

Maybe you just get overwhelmed by the apparent enormity of things, or your life just feels too full and busy to squeeze anything else in?

There are many reasons why we settle for what we have, most have their roots in fear in one form or another and most are deeply unconscious.

We make lots of excuses to ourselves to cover those deep seated fears. Things like:

* I don't have time

* I can't afford it

* It's not possible

* That's not for people like me

* It's too hard

* I don't know how

* My friends will laugh at me

* My family won't like it

* I don't want to be like the other people who have/do that

The list goes on and on.

But here's the thing.

That list of reasons why you couldn't or shouldn't do the things you'd love to, they're all lies.

They're all just unconscious excuses you've come up with to keep yourself safe. Safe from feeling rejected; safe from the risk of failure and disappointment.

They help your life to fulfil, **but not exceed**, your expectations and keep you within the relative safety of your comfort zone – which ironically may actually be anything but comfortable!

It's not fun being so broke you can't go out or buy new things and have to worry about paying your bills. It's no fun looking at your out of shape reflection with loathing because yet another diet has failed.

It's no fun staying home again because nobody invited you to the party everyone else seems to be going to.

This reality is no fun at all! But it might well be familiar. It's what you've grown accustomed to and learnt to expect and accept.

Unfortunately, as well as keeping you safe, these restrictions are also keeping you from leading the life of your dreams.

You are making a prison in your mind and acting as your own jailor!

Is that really a good exchange?

It's like living your life in greyscale when it could be rainbow coloured; listening to the same flat note over and over, when you could be listening to an overture played by gifted musicians; wearing cold, damp clothes in the snow when you could be kitted out in the warmest, softest most luxurious ski kit.

Why would you?

Surely you must know that you're worth more than that, even if you don't know how to go get it just yet?

~~~

Making Resolutions

They said the road to hell is paved with good intentions and in many ways, that's exactly what resolutions are.

Making resolutions is practically an international pass time these days. So much so, that we could almost propose it as a new Olympic sport, along with those other greats like *procrastination* and *giving up* things which are bad for us! We find cues all over the place that convince us we need to make a change, but they are rarely permanent.

As we watch the passing of another year, feeling perhaps nostalgic about the things it has brought, or indeed taken from us, during its passage, we think about how we might do things differently next year.

At lent, even non-believers give something up for a few weeks, usually to take it up again as soon as the prescribed time is up.

Maybe we experience a 'wake-up call', or witness an event in someone else's life which spurs us into action for a short while.

Like diets that will start, and bad habits that will end, *'next week'*, we are fuelled by rocket like enthusiasm and may spend some considerable time moulding these good intentions. We work out how we will fit them into our lives, what changes we'll make in order to make them possible. We decide what we'll stop doing and what we'll start and think of all the ways in which our life will be improved if we stick to our guns this time.

No matter how well meant or painstakingly crafted however, many of these resolutions will contain more *dissolve* than *resolve*, and will have faded by the next change of season.

Why is it then, that year after year, we go through the same process, swearing blindly that *'this time I will stick to it'*?

Don't we know in our hearts that within a few weeks or months, these new resolutions will have been condemned to the same dark recesses of our mind as the ones we broke last year, and the year before?

Of course we know, and yet we go through the same ritual – sometimes more than once a year – preparing a set of excuses why we just couldn't stick to it this time and reasons why it will be different next time!

~~~

Why Resolutions Don't Last

There are a number of reasons why the vast majority of New Year's Resolutions are doomed to fail before the clock strikes 12 and other equally well meant decisions never achieve their outcome.

Their failure is largely down to your unconscious incongruence. All this means is, that while you consciously want the things you say, you are unconsciously running patterns and holding beliefs that are working against you.

For example, a common theme for resolutions is getting fit and losing weight. You might decide you want to get fitter and thinner and come up with a whole list of reasons why this would be great and really mean them. But if, at a deeply unconscious level, you have the belief that you will never be thin or have the body you want, you will sabotage your own attempts and prevent yourself from reaching your goals.

You may have a hidden fear of rejection for example, and use being overweight as a protection strategy, as it gives you a reason to explain why you don't have a partner or as many friends as other people you know. You may hide your fear of meeting new people behind your muffin top and avoid social gatherings all together.

With such deep rooted fears and beliefs, your conscious desires don't stand a chance. It's like a paper boat trying to beat an ocean current.

You might consciously think you want to be successful in your business and make lots of money, but what if you have an unconscious belief that rich people are dishonest, or unhappy? – two very common conceptions which are hardly surprising given the amount of both of these types of people we are bombarded with in the media – would you really want to be actively working towards something that would make you unhappy? No, of course not! So your unconscious will step in and make sure you avoid the risk of unhappiness. Unfortunately that also means you won't be rich or successful, but they were only conscious wants anyway and the unconscious ones always win!

~~~

Why Goals Are Different

The great news is, there are some really easy ways to make this time different.

This time, you are going to create some really specific, individual goals or outcomes that you can stick to, instead of making vague, hopeful promises to yourself.

You are going to conceive the most wonderful, exciting and compelling future that will pull you into it and leave you almost powerless to resist!

A future that will give you all you truly desire - be that money, love, freedom, friendship, better fitness levels, a smaller waist line or anything else you can think of. A new house, a new job, more time to spend with your family, less stress, better relationships, a great holiday; the list is only limited by your imagination.

You are going to do this in such a way that not only will you know that you want this consciously, but you will engage your unconscious mind to want it too. This means instead of the conscious 10% of your brain battling it out against the powerhouse 90% unconscious, 100% of you will be fighting for you! Doesn't that sound more like a winning team? No more tug of war, it'll be all tug and all for you!

~~~

The Formula for Success

Does having a perfect life sound like something you might enjoy?

Could you do with more abundance in some area of your life?

Do you get a buzz at the thought of waking up feeling excited about the day to come on a regular basis?

Have you got a whole list of things you want to accomplish? If so, then read on!

Whilst we express our formula for success in slightly different ways - Chris and Susan have their **BLT and Fries**

and despite never having understood maths terribly well at school, Amanda favours a mock equation,

Success = Activity (Mindset + System)

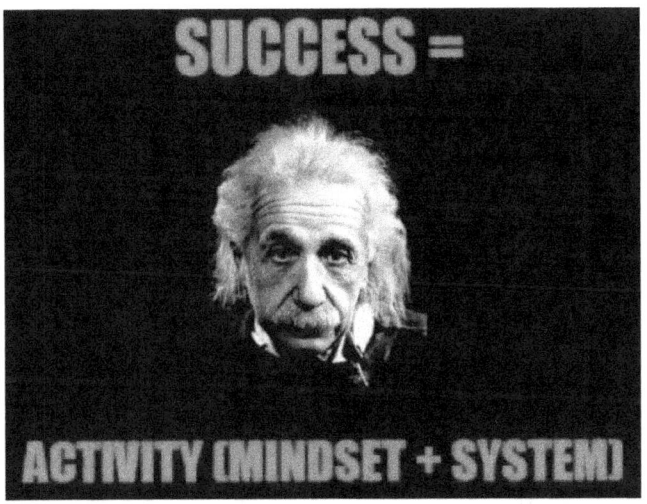

- we all agree on the basic ingredients for creating success in any area is very simple!

If you have the right **mindset,** which includes a strong belief in yourself and belief that it's possible, a willingness to learn and be teachable and are prepared to take consistent, focused action (**Activity**) you **will be successful**.

And that applies to everyone and in every area of life! **That means you!**

This book will provide you with a system to follow that will cultivate your mindset in the process. You already have the potential, so all you have to do is put in the effort and commit to a little regular (and easy) activity!

~~~

Step 1
Change Your Thinking

Bad habits are often where we look when we start thinking about making resolutions or creating goals. We want to lose weight or stop smoking, to get fitter or stop biting our nails and yet the way we think about these things in our mind works against us.

The law of attraction works by giving you what you are focusing on – matching things to your thoughts and bringing them into your reality.

So, if for example, your focus is on not having enough time to do what you want, you will always have not enough time. If you are worrying about not having enough money to pay the bills, you will continue to have a shortage to worry about. If you are fixated on a lack of something in your life, you will attract more 'lack'.

You need to learn to reformulate, or reframe, the way you think about things.

Decide how much money you want to earn and focus on that. Tell yourself that you are worth that much and more. Affirmations are a great tool for helping these thoughts become beliefs.

Think about what your ideal day might look like and focus on creating that. Think about the attributes you want to be known for and practice them. You might want to feel like you did at a previous moment in your life, - a time when you were successful or confident for example. If so focus on that, and remember, if you have achieved that before you can easily do so again! You have already proved it is possible for you, so believing it is so should be much easier.

Don't think about *giving up* something. Think instead about the benefits that not doing *that* anymore will give you.

Smoking is a favourite. We think about *giving up smoking* and yet what does that actually mean?

* *Giving up* endangering our own life and the lives of others with the toxic smoke?

* *Giving up* the horrid smell on our clothes, possessions, body and breath?

* *Giving up* literally sending money up in smoke?

We focus on the short term pain that chemical and psychological withdrawal will cause and not the numerous gains and it doesn't feel very compelling does it!

Think instead about becoming someone who used to smoke; who smells fresh; is healthy and of never having that awful feeling of needing a cigarette again.

The secret is to focus on the long term positive benefits of not smoking, not the short term pain of withdrawal. It's just the other side of the coin but it's much more motivating and appeals to your positive nature to succeed.

Apply the same logic to creating your new life. Think about how much easier life will be when you have created a successful business. Focus on the things you will be able to do, the way you will feel about yourself, the way you will behave, the things you will think about. Forget about the time you will have to contribute to the set up of your business. You're not giving up watching TV, going to the pub or chatting on Facebook aimlessly. You're making a positive choice to spend your time in a way that will benefit you and take you closer to your goals.

~~~

Examples

We've all been through this process ourselves so we can speak with some authority.

Amanda had 'given up smoking' for long periods many times and always gone back to it, until 2010. This time, she changed her beliefs about herself, set the goal of being a non-smoker, and stopped – just like that. And she has never even had a puff since. Not once has the thought of taking a cigarette crossed her mind. Even the physical withdrawal didn't bother her – and she'd been a 20 a day smoker for most of her adult life.

She says "Now the thought of smoking is as distasteful and alien as the idea of taking Heroin. Smoking is just not something that I do now. I am a non-smoker, end of story!"

Similarly, we wanted to write a book about our common experiences. We didn't know how to go about it at first but we set ourselves the goal and worked towards it one step at a time, doing the work necessary and holding each other accountable. The book you are reading now is our second joint venture, so you see it can be done!

We all wanted to speak about our experiences and our passions and that's another goal we've realised. We are no different to you. We have our challenges just like you do, so before you think it's been any easier for us than it will be for you, stop. Stop telling yourself those stories and giving yourself those excuses. Save the energy and put it towards creating your perfect life instead.

Be honest and don't short change yourself. Think about what you <u>really</u> want and not a watered down version!

Although you may not yet know how to *achieve* your goal, that's not your problem. The laws of attraction and your unconscious mind will work on that, as long as you remain focussed. The opportunities will come and if you are looking out for what you want and are prepared to take action when they do, you will succeed.

You cannot consciously conceive what you haven't yet experienced, or at least heard of, so don't limit yourself to only what you already know. Allow yourself to dream. The bigger and bolder, the better!

~~~

Step 2
Decide Where to Start

To begin with you are going to decide on the outcome you want to achieve, (or set of outcomes, but start with one) and you are going to do this in a very specific and deliberate way. This will allow you to overcome any unconscious barriers and set your unconscious mind to work at top speed, with the fewest number of obstacles possible, to get your outcome.

You may already know where you want to begin and what would have the biggest impact on your life, if it were improved. If you're not sure where to start, or what to tackle next, this next exercise will help you decide. Remember though, that there are no right or wrong answers. As long as it's right for you, it's right!

~~~

Choosing Your Key Life Areas

Exercise

Remember these are only examples, go with whatever feels right for you.

* Health

* Career

* Money/Financial Position

* Family/Friends

* Spirituality

* Relationships

* Fun/hobbies/leisure

* Personal Development

Give yourself a score out of 10 as to how satisfied you are in each area to help you decide.

If you find that you have several which score highly and need attention, ask yourself,

'If I had 10 on this one, could the others wait?'

'Would resolving this have the biggest and best impact on my life?'

This isn't a one off process, you get to go back time and time again and work on as many things as you want to and believe me, when you get good at this and see great results, that's exactly what you'll want to do!

Remember that in the universe there are no limits and no lack.

There is no shortage of money. There is enough currency in the world for us all to have a million pounds each, it's just a distribution issue, not a shortage.

There is no shortage of people and prospective friends and lovers in the world. You just have to be in the right place, at the right time and with confidence and an openness of mind to spot and act upon the potential.

There is no reason why something you want cannot be yours, if you are willing to invest the time and energy it takes to get it.

You just have to find a system, cultivate the right mindset and take action again and again until you are where you want to be.

~~~

Step 3
Decide Specifically What You Want

Having thought a bit about which area of your life that you'd like to improve, you next need to think about what it is specifically that you'd like to change, and why.

All the things we yearn for in life, as practical and tangible as they might seem, ultimately lead to a positive emotion. We want to improve our lives to feel better.

You might want more money for example and have a list as long as your arm of the things you'll buy with it, but if you look at the list and ask yourself

'Why do I want that?'

'For what purpose?'

You will very quickly notice that owning those things is just a means to an emotional end. Either it will make you feel better about something or it will make someone you care about feel better.

Try it and see!

If your main goal is a financial one, instead of thinking about a figure, think about what achieving that goal will give you and how it will feel. I.e. if you want more money to buy a bigger house, what will having that new house give you? – space, relaxation and freedom perhaps? Imagine how you will feel when you are sitting inside it. The key thing here is that the money is not the motivation, just the means to achieving what you want.

~~~

Step 4

The Construction Process

Once you've decided on your area of focus, the next thing you're going to do, is daydream! Not so hard to do - you dream every night (even if you don't remember when you wake up) and often while you're awake too. This is going to be constructive dreaming though, like making a movie in your head. You are going to pick an area of your life that you want to improve and then dream about it! – but not just yet...

Why Dream?

There are several great reasons why this is the best way to begin this process. The first point is that it's very important to focus on what it is that you want and not on what you don't want. As humans, we are often much better at describing what we don't want to happen than what we do want.

~~~

Example

Imagine that you have a job you hate (unfortunately for many people this is a reality).

If we were to ask you what you would like to change and how you would prefer things to be, what would you say? You may find a whole list of things that you would want not to have in new job;

'I want to work less hours'

'I don't want to commute any more'

'I wouldn't want to work with my current boss'

'I don't want so much responsibility'

'Anything as long as it's not that!' etc

And whilst all these statements may be true, you need to turn this thinking around and find the flip side of the coin.

The reason for this is very simple.

Your unconscious, which will be crucial in helping you attain the goals you set yourself, doesn't process negatives. So when you say *'I don't want x'*, it hears *'I want x'* and sets about getting it for you. It will filter your experience (the things you notice, see, hear, feel etc) to support this. You can find lots more about this in Volume 3 of Amanda's Self Help Bible series if you are interested. If you just want the short version then this is it. What you think about most often will appear in your life.

The law of attraction works in the same way by matching your reality to your predominant thoughts. There's a lot of talk about the law of attraction these days and how easy it is to use it to get what you want in life. It's true that if you learn to leverage it correctly the law of attraction will help you no end. But beware! Just like your unconscious, it's very literal. There is no judgement, or reasoning, or working it out, you think about being poor, you'll attract more ways to experience that feeling. You concentrate on the fact that you don't yet know how to do something and you'll find plenty more to keep you confused. Keep telling yourself that it will never work for you and guess what... you're getting the idea by now!

The one thing that's missing from much of the current wave of teaching on the LOA, is that it still requires effort on your part. You still have to be prepared to act upon the opportunities and advantages that come your way. You also need to be open minded. Success may not happen the way you expect it to, so be prepared! Don't miss out on a short cut just because it doesn't look like you thought it would!

The second equally important point is also linked to your focus, only this time it's about the direction.

Imagine your life is a train track with a station at each end. One station, let's call it 'Station A', represents the thing that you want, and the other, 'Station B', houses the thing you are trying to escape.

A ◄──────────────────────► B

Whether you are moving away from station B and what you don't want, or towards station A, you will move in the <u>same</u> direction. BUT if you are thinking about moving away from Station B, you will be focusing on that and whatever it is that you are trying to escape. You are basically being driven by your fear. Whilst you may move quickly at first, propelled by your desire to get away from B, as you get further your away your motivation and momentum will decline, because the fear drops the further away you get. Often this leads to a little crisis. You may have just begun to feel safe and all of a sudden BANG! You're right back where you started or doing the famous 'one step forward, two steps back.

At best your progress will slow until you're almost back where you started and then you'll get re-motivated and repel yourself!

There are lots of obvious examples of this in real life, yo-yo diets, people like Donald Trump who go through life constantly making great fortunes only to lose them and have to start all over again.

If, on the other hand, you turn your back on B, A will remain firmly in your focus and you will automatically be pulled towards it. Your motivation will now be for reaching A, so the closer you get, the faster you'll go and you won't stop until you're there! Isn't that better?

Another equally important point, and great reason for spending time daydreaming, is that your unconscious cannot tell the difference between something that happens for real and something you imagine or just see in your mind. That's why nightmares are so scary, books so all consuming and anxiety such a horrific impediment.

By imagining your life as you want it to be, you'll engage your unconscious to start looking out for ways to get you to that point and set the filters which choose what to let through to your conscious awareness onto the right path.

You'll also start attracting the things, people and situations that can help you into your life, rather than more of what you don't want.

So, this next step is to make a movie in your head of a very particular scenario, which we'll explain shortly, and then you're going to write about it.

Before we give you the scenario for this visualisation, you need to consider some very important factors, as this will help you make sure you include everything you need to first time round. These are the key to creating a compelling goal. You might like to think of them like the ingredients in a recipe and they are what make the difference between a goal that works and a resolution that doesn't.

~~~

The Keys to a Compelling Goal

Be Clear About Why You Want This

Exercise

Start by asking yourself the following questions and record your answers. Seeing things written down in black and white will help you make sense of them, help them embed in your unconscious and start the process of commitment that you're going to need.

a) What will achieving this allow me to do?

b) What will I be able to stop doing or avoid?

c) What will happen if I don't get this?

d) What won't happen if I don't get this?

e) How will I feel when I get it?

f) What will my life look like when I've got it?

What will you see, hear and feel, when you have this? Imagine yourself in the future, after you've achieved this goal and think about it as though it were now.

~~~

Know How You'll Know When You Have It

Exercise

Here are some questions that you'll need to be able to answer once you've made your movie, so write them down now and it will help to remind you of what you need to look out for. If once you've made your movie you realise that you didn't include enough detail to get the answers to these questions, don't worry, just sit back and day dream for a few minutes longer until you get them!

As ever, there are no right or wrong answers, go with what comes to you and trust your unconscious mind to give you the best answers for you. This is a personal journey you are making here.

a) How did you feel when you got it?

b) What specifically had changed?

c) What had to happen so that you knew you had achieved your goal?

* Was it a feeling you got that let you know that you'd achieved your aim?

* Was it hearing someone else acknowledge it, or perhaps that voice inside your head that told you you'd done really well?

* Was it finally ticking off the last of a long list of 'To do's'?

* Was it something you saw? The look on someone's face? Your own happy reflection? More 0's on a bank statement or pay cheque? That completed list?

* Was it something you experienced? The time to do something you couldn't previously perhaps? A good night's sleep? A holiday?

~~~

Think Through All Consequences

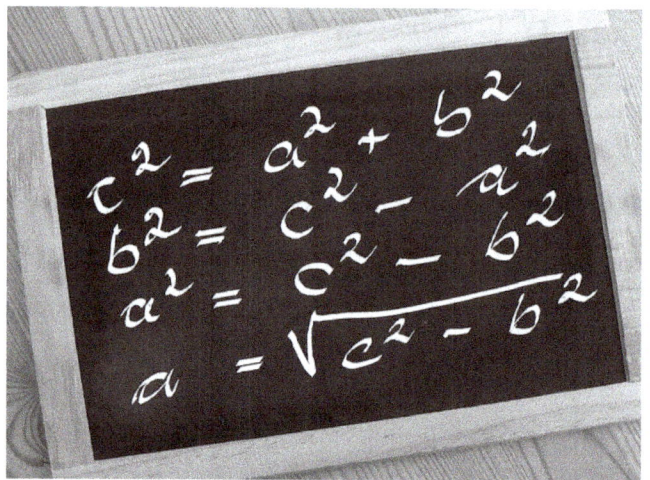

What will this outcome get for you, or allow you to do? What will have to change for you to have this?

It might mean you can no longer do something, or have to do something else instead. Go back over the questions in point 2 and check that having this won't be detrimental to you or anyone else important to you.

~~~

Be Clear About <u>What</u> and <u>Who</u> Is Involved In Your Goal

Where, when, how and with whom, do you want to get it? You probably don't live in total isolation, so be clear if anyone else is implicated in your goal.

It's fine if someone else will benefit from it as a result of you achieving your goal, or if you want to share your success with someone else, but in order to be fully engaged at both a conscious and unconscious level, you must make sure that essentially it is only for you and **must not <u>depend</u> on any one else to help you achieve it.**

Everybody has their own issues, desires, commitments and restrictions and life changes us all the time. Don't let your goal slip away from you by relying on someone else to help get it.

When you give the responsibility for achieving your goals away, you give away your power to achieve them too.

Giving even part of the responsibility to someone else leaves room for blame, disappointment and excuses. Keep the power where it belongs, with you, by being accountable to yourself 100%.

Why do you want this? What will you gain or lose if you have it? What are the positive benefits for you and everyone else implicated.

It must be something that is good for you– i.e. it wouldn't be good for you to have a goal to weigh only 5 stone, or something that might harm you.

It mustn't be something that might harm or disadvantage anyone else either. Remember, even if you don't believe in the idea of universal karma, or the law of attraction, if you are focusing on something unpleasant happening to someone else, your unconscious will be taking it personally, as though you were wishing it for yourself AND it will do it's best to bring things into your reality in line with your thinking. That's just the way your brain is wired, you become consciously aware of the things that match your predominant thoughts and it's those things that form your perception and therefore your reality.

~~~

Setting the Scene

The Checklist

Once you can answer yes to all the following questions, you can go ahead and prepare for your visualisation or dream session.

1) Have you chosen the area of your life that you are going to work on and improve with this fantastic, life changing goal now?

2) Are you clear about exactly what you want?

3) Have you got a good understanding of why you want this goal and what it will mean to you at an emotional level?

4) Do you know what will have to happen for you to realise that you have achieved this goal?

5) Have you thoroughly considered all the consequences of you reaching this goal?

6) Are you clear about who and what will be involved in your goal?

Now, I want you to imagine that moment in the future, when you realise that you have accomplished the goal you are about to construct.

It might be a social gathering, celebration or other significant occasion; It might be a much more formal or private realisation. Whatever you think would be most appropriate and above all, what would give you the most pleasure.

If you are constructing a goal that revolves around your business, you might imagine being awarded a key contract and the meeting that delivers the news. Or perhaps the moment that you are able to tell your workforce or significant other the good news.

Chris and Susan had a goal whereby they saw themselves receiving one of those oversized cheques on stage at an Empower Network event. If you've seen anything of their journey, you'll know that by Summer 2013 they'd achieved that twice.

Amanda wanted to publish books that would help people to make positive changes in their lives. She now regularly receives the emails she visualised from people telling her how she's helped them.

The three of us have lots of goals yet to be realised. Remember that this is an ongoing process and you get to keep adding to the list as you go and we can promise you, that as soon as you start to see the things you planned coming to fruition, you'll be champing at the bit to add to that list with even bigger, more exciting and audacious things!

The choice is only limited by your imagination.

Example

The vision for one of Amanda's big personal goals focuses around the moment she closes the front door in a new, bigger house.

"I can hear the swoosh of the door across the polished floor, and the clunk of the door as it shuts. I can feel the pattern of the door under my hands and the warmth of the wood on my back as I lean against it. I can hear my sigh of relief and contentment as I realise that this is the moment I have been waiting for.

Even as I think of it I find myself smiling and a warm glow creep over me."

The key is in knowing and experiencing how we will *feel* in that moment. The other senses add to the realism of the goal and increase the desire to achieve it.

So as you build your dream, we want you to notice some very specific things.

* How does it feel to have achieved this goal? What does it feel like to finally have this great life?

* What do you look like? What does your body language say about you? What are you wearing?

* Who else is there? As well as creating an image of <u>what</u> you want to have in this dream life, we want you to imagine <u>who</u> will be there with you. Who do you want to be there to share your joy? Whose presence will make it even more special?

* What can you hear around you? Are there any important sounds? Can you imagine what lovely things other people are saying about you? What are you saying to yourself?

*Are there any smells associated with this moment?

This dream session should be fun, it should fill you with hope and joy and desire to make it all real, so lie back and enjoy it!

Find a nice quiet spot and some time where you won't be disturbed. Set your dreaming up like a treat or a special time, get excited about it. You might like some soft lighting or music that appeals to you, or you might like to be in a special place. Whatever works for you is just fine. Just put as much effort into this as you can and put lots of detail into your dream.

~~~

Step 5

Write It All Down

Once you've enjoyed creating this epic moment in your mind, you are going to write it all down. Not just in a haphazard kind of way though. This is too important for that so you're going to follow some easy guidelines.

Write a story because they work really well and it's easy to include lots of details. Stories engage our imagination and speak to us at a deeply metaphorical level.

You don't need to be the next Shakespeare, this is for you and about you, so you're the very best person to do it. Writing it down is the best way to clarify exactly what you want to achieve and having it will act as a convenient reminder of the decision you have made.

So here are the golden rules you have to stick to as you get ready to write it all down.

~~~

Start by specifying your present situation

Pick a date in the future by which time you want to have arrived at Station A, and achieved your goal and begin your story by stating what the date is, because you want to achieve this and not for it to be forever in the future!

Begin your story as though you are looking back from that date in the future to now and describe remembering or recalling where you are now. This is your start point and a springboard for your imagination. This doesn't need to be gloomy or lengthy, just enough to draw a nice contrast with where you are going.

Example

It is the 5th of July 2014 (this is the date by which I want to achieve this goal) *and as I look back to September 2013, I remember…*

~~~

Be Specific

* What **specifically** do you want?

Focus on what you <u>do</u> want, as opposed to what you <u>don't</u> want.

Instead of saying that you don't want to be hard up anymore, or just want more money, say that you want to be financially secure for life, or have enough money to pay all your bills and have x amount left over every month.

Write about that <u>specific</u> time that you imagined and exactly what you are doing, feeling, seeing and hearing, to make a really exciting, tempting outcome.

Describe your dream, including all of the things you took care to include. The people who are there with you, the things you see and hear and the wonderful positive emotions you feel in that moment as you realise that you have achieved this goal.

If you want a new house, describe it in detail, how big are the rooms, what style is the house, what is the location like? What does this signify for you, who is there to share your joy and complete the picture?

The more detail you can give, the better the goal will be embedded in your unconscious mind and the more sure it will seem.

It is important to add as much detail as possible in order to make it as desirable and realistic as you can. After all, this is your future, so make it the most compelling future that you can and think big – the bigger the better!

~~~

Mind Your Language!

Toxic

Your words create your world – quite literally! They create your thoughts, which create your behaviour and your perception of the world, so use them wisely.

* Make sure there are no negatives in there - things like no, none, don't, can't, won't etc

Remember that your unconscious won't process them so you'll just be calling out for what you don't want!

* Avoid neutral, wishy-washy words like nice, good,

Would you like a 'nice' house or a 'sensational' one? A 'good' job or 'the most fantastic job ever'? Find some really juicy words to spice it up!

* Avoid words like 'more', 'better', 'less'

If I gave you $10 you'd have **more** money than you do now but it wouldn't change your life would it? If you had two **more** clients, would that be enough? If not state how many you'd like; 2 new clients a day... 100 clients a year... etc

If your boss cut your working hours by 1 a week, you'd be working (and as a consequence earning) **less** but it's unlikely to make a significant difference to your week.

You might start out by thinking I want less of X or more of Y and that's fine, just make sure you switch round from the negative side now and get specific.

~~~

Enjoy the Process

If you've done the first part of this exercise well and created a really vibrant dream, all you need to do is describe it! This will be easy!

~~~

Step 6
Follow It Up

What Next?
Tools to Help Your Progress

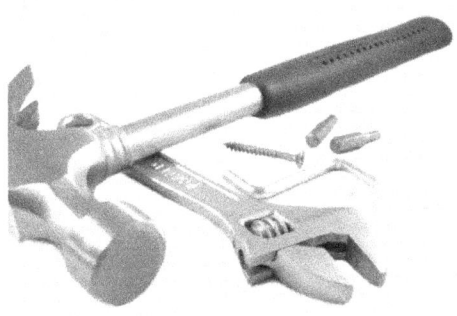

Once you have written this goal down, you have completed the first step and laid the foundation of your success. But having this story written down will not materialise your goal all by itself. Shame we know!

Now you need to really get this goal into your focus and there are lots of ways you can do this.

1) Get into the habit of reading it aloud to yourself, first thing in the morning and last thing at night ideally. Stick it up somewhere you can see it and carry it around with you so that you can read it when you get a quiet moment.

This repetition will start to embed it in your mind and help you to notice the things which will begin appearing in your life that will lead you on the path towards your goal.

Like Hansel and Gretel following the trail of breadcrumbs, you will begin to find little things popping up in your life that will help you. You will find yourself looking at old situations and people in a new light. They will either fit in with your new direction or you'll see that perhaps they were part of what kept you where you were before. Then it's up to you what you decide to do about it. **The thing with changing your life – is that you change your life!** And that can mean leaving some things behind and you need to know that it's ok.

Life is a fluid and evolving thing and as your life evolves, it may carve a path that's only wide enough for you at some points, but it is still your path and you must find the courage to walk it. You may find that when it widens out again, there will be room for others and then you can walk with anyone you choose to and the people you find then will be heading in the same direction as you.

2) Never allow <u>your</u> path to be blocked by the fear, or lack of ambition of another, because that pathway will only ever end in regret and disappointment.

3) Hold yourself accountable. Keeping a journal is a great idea. Make a record of what you've done each day towards your goal. Note down the things you notice, the new opportunities that appear and each step you take.

4) If you are worried that you won't be a strict enough task master, get an accountability buddy. This might be someone with a similar goal to yours – this works really well with health and fitness related goals. It could be a partner or loved one, but pick someone who won't let you off if you stray from the track!

Or, if you want to go the whole hog, get yourself a coach.

Goal setting is one of the first things most coaches will talk to you about because it's part of their role to make sure that you stick to them! If you want something badly enough to go to the effort of creating a goal around it, it's got to be worth sticking to surely!

Use tools which will work on your unconscious for you.

5) Affirmations and further visualisations are great tools which are easy to fit into any schedule and work really well in helping get your mindset ready for your goal. If you'd like some help with affirmations, go to http://bit.ly/makingaffirmations where you'll find some posts Amanda has written to help you.

6) Dream or vision boards are a fantastic visual reminder of what you want and why. You can create separate boards for different goals or one big one that captures them all. It's up to you.

7) Subliminal messaging is another powerful too. This can be done using a programme that hides written messages and flashes them up on your computer so quickly that your eye doesn't even notice them, or as audio messages hidden under white noise or other sounds.

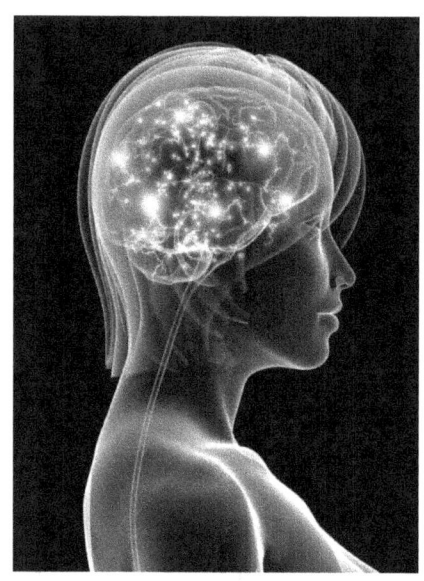

Amanda loves listening to subliminal messages hidden under the sounds of the ocean, perhaps it's an association to growing up by the sea. You can find some **free downloads of the subliminal messages she uses here** http://bit.ly/QZPFOm

8) On that same page you'll also find some great hypnosis tracks you can download for free. If you have yet to try hypnosis, then we'd highly recommend it. It will help iron out the creases in your mind with a complete lack of effort on your part!

9) Think about what resources you need. Think about what you have now and what you might need to get this goal and then find out how you can bridge the gap.

Have you ever had or done this before or do you know anyone who has? If so, how and with what did you or they achieve it? Learn from your previous and other people's mistakes and successes.

Don't think it will be better if you forge ahead alone and make your own mistakes because it won't. You'll just be slowing your own progress down and let's face it, if you knew the answers already, wouldn't you be living that life right now?

Look for things, people and information that will help you get there in the shortest time and the most direct way.

If there are things that you want to achieve and you don't know how, that doesn't mean you can never achieve them. It just means you don't know how *yet*! Just like you didn't know how to ride a bike before you learnt!

It may be that you don't know how you'll find out either at this stage, but once you get this goal written and really begin some focused activity on it, things will come into your life seemingly from nowhere, to bring you the answers and the tools you need.

You may have heard the phrase,

"When the student is ready, the teacher will appear"

Well, get to work and you'll soon see it's true!

If you know how the unconscious mind works in creating your perspective and your reality, you'll already understand why, once you are really focused, you cannot help but get what you want.

If you don't know how that works, then read 'How to Change Reality. The Unconscious & The Communication Process', Volume 3 of Amanda's Self Help Bible series.

10) Never give up.

This is perhaps the most important point of all. Be persistent.

There will always be a tiny part of you that will expect you to 'cave in', 'give up' or just 'fail' and that little part will pipe up in its whiny *'I told you so'* little voice every time you are low, or feel like you can't be bothered today! It'll offer you excuses and reasons why it would be ok to give up now, but don't listen! Tell it to shut up and butt out because this time, you're in charge!

Whatever you decide to do in life, there will be times where things don't go to plan and you may even feel like you have failed on occasion. But, if you can pick yourself up, analyse the situation to see what went wrong, learn and move forward, you will not have failed.

Nothing is impossible if you want it enough and are prepared to keep going until you achieve it.

See each setback as a lesson; learn what it has to teach you and do something differently the next time.

If you don't reach your goal by the date you specified, keep going. Think about it this way, which is more important, getting there by that specific date, or just getting there?

If it takes you a few weeks or months longer to achieve that huge, wonderful thing you're thinking about, will it really matter? In 10 years time, as you look back, do you think it will be worse to think "Well I didn't have that dream house by the 5th of July like I said I would, so I gave up" or to say to yourself, "Well it took me a few months longer than I thought, but I kept going and got the house I'd dreamed of"?

We know which would bother us more!

Knowing exactly what you want and why will really motivate you and you'll find that your frame of mind will become increasingly positive and the path that you are following will become clearer, the longer that you stick at it.

New opportunities will come, new people aligned with where you are heading and new indicators that you're on the right track.

Creating your own success begins with knowing what that success actually is for you. Keep up the focused and consistent action, learn from every opportunity and practice self belief until it no longer requires thought and your mindset will become laser sharp, propelling you toward to your ultimate and inevitable Success!

~~~

About the Authors

Amanda Ollier

This is the 7th book I've written in the past couple of years, something that's been a goal of mine for a very long time! In the end, I had to listen to my own advice, stop waiting until I had enough time, focus on what I really wanted to achieve and just get on with it. So you see, when I tell you that setting proper goals works, I speak from experience!

I've been studying personal development in one form or another for over 20 years now and am a Master Practitioner of NLP (neuro-linguistic programming), amongst other things.

I've tried lots of different things during my life and now happily concentrate on writing, coaching and speaking, all of which I love.

I understand that the most successful people in all walks of life, whether that be in business, sport or relationships, all first devoted time to their own self development. Knowing where to start is often the hardest thing and realising what your strengths are can be tough. I enjoy helping people to do both of those and hope that my books will give you the head start and momentum that you need.

I am also the proud mother to two fantastic boys, who continue to amaze and delight me and inspire me to keep going. They're my 'why' and when I feel like I want to put something off until tomorrow, or give up altogether, it's their faces that I see urging me on. I hope your 'why' will motivate you in the same wonderful way!

~~~

Chris and Susan Beesley

We are both from a professional background as accountants and management consultants and have owned and run our own businesses since 1983, so making a change from the traditional *"time for money"* way of life was as much a change for us, as it most likely is for you as you are reading this.

The seed was sown for us ten years ago when we discovered network marketing and came to understand that there were alternative ways to make money other than the traditional job income. We set ourselves the goal of working online full time.

Whilst our first foray into that market was not as successful in monetary terms as we expected, what we learnt forms the basis of our business today - principally the importance of leverage and building a residual income. The same formula that the most prosperous people in the world use to create their wealth - people like Robert Kiyosaki and Donald Trump to name but a few.

Fast forward to 2009, in our fifties, we realised that time was marching on, the children had left home and we hadn't yet achieved our dream to travel the world and especially to spend a whole season pursuing our passion of skiing (everyone has to have a reason why). We knew that if we continued to "**work**" our management consultancy, the only way we could generate more income was to work longer hours and that wasn't going to happen!

Long story short - we don't have a '*rags to riches*' story; we have not been addicted to alcohol or drugs, been homeless or anything like that - but one particular event in our business led us to know that we had to make a change in our lives if we were to '*live our dream*'. It will be the same for you.

As a result of that event we set about researching a way that we could do that. A way which would fulfil our criteria - we wanted to be able to work from home, or anywhere in the world (passion for travel). This naturally led us to the internet and the decision to work online. Of course your criteria may be very different to ours, that doesn't matter, as you long as you know what your reason why is.

What a minefield that was! Everywhere you looked people appeared to be making serious amounts of money from various online business opportunities. Our challenge, just like yours was "*Is it real?*", "*Who can you trust?*", "*Can I do it?*" We can tell you that we made some mistakes and were seduced by some very clever people hiding behind well written sales pages - what we now call 'the internet magicians'. We bought plenty of shiny objects (ADOS!), what we now famously call *'Shelf Development'* products, because they never get any further than the shelf! You will undoubtedly do the same or have done the same. We learnt from that just like Amanda did. You will learn from it as well - maybe you already have! The best advice we can give is to do what we call in accountant speak your '*due diligence*'. That means research diligently what is being offered. *Does it align with your personal values, passion or experience. Can you contact someone? Can you speak to a real person? Have they achieved the success you desire?*

We would also advise that you don't just go and quit your job; that you build your new home business part time. This gives you the financial security of knowing you have one stream of income whilst you develop another.

This is exactly what we did - so that in six months of working our management consultancy full time and building our home business online part time we were able to make the switch and in so doing achieve our goal.

Connect With the Authors Online

If you'd like to get in touch, we'd love to hear from you!

You can find us collectively at

www.themindsetshift.com

...or on Facebook at

www.facebook.com/themindsetshift

...you can email Chris and Susan at:

info@chrisandsusanbeesley.com

...and Amanda at:

Amanda@theselfhelpbible.com

~~~

Other Books We've Written

Amanda, Chris and Susan have other books you might enjoy. Read about The Mindset Shift – From Employee to Home Business Entrepreneur and see where you can buy the version that best suits your needs here

www.themindsetshift.com

Amanda also writes personal development books called The Self Help Bible and educational books for children. You can see more on them at

www.amazon.com/author/amandaollier

~~~

….And Finally

We hope that you will use what you've read here to create yourself some really compelling goals now and make the coming year the best you've ever had.

At some point in our lives, most of us are reminded of how short life can be and that we should make the most of every day and yet we often don't do that.

Don't let life get in your way again, take some time out to think about what you really want your future to look like and then make the time to do something about it. If you wait to have 'spare' or 'enough' time, you'll wait forever!

As well as leading you on to a bigger and brighter future, well constructed goals can really give you a feeling of hope, a sense of empowerment and the momentum to keep you going.

In the age of 'designer this' and 'designer that' why not give yourself the gift of a 'designer future', created by the perfect designer for your life – YOU!

Remember:

Your past does not equal your future. What comes next is up to you!

If you enjoyed this book, we'd really appreciate it if you could post a review back on Amazon.

~~~

www.ingramcontent.com/pod-product-compliance
Lightning Source LLC
Chambersburg PA
CBHW071801200526
45167CB00017B/962